Jewish Activity Book

Jill Dubin

DOVER PUBLICATIONS, INC.
New York

Published in Canada by General Publishing Company, Ltd., 30 Les-
mill Road, Don Mills, Toronto, Ontario.
Published in the United Kingdom by Constable and Company, Ltd.,
3 The Lanchesters, 162–164 Fulham Palace Road, London W6 9ER.

Jewish Activity Book is a new work, first published by Dover Publications, Inc., in 1992.

International Standard Book Number: 0-486-27257-5

Manufactured in the United States of America
Dover Publications, Inc., 31 East 2nd Street, Mineola, N.Y. 11501

Note

The 41 games and puzzles in this book include: cross-words, mazes, follow-the-dots, hidden pictures, color-by-number, search-a-word, scrambled words, counting, what's-wrong-with-this-picture, find-the-look-alikes, differences between pictures, and more!

The activities are all concerned with Jewish life: holiday celebrations (Passover, Purim, Rosh Hashonah, Sukkot, Chanukah), religious objects and symbols (Torah, shofar, menorah, Star of David), Bible stories (Tree of Life, Noah), favorite foods (bagel, latke, matzo, hamantash) and many other aspects of Jewishness.

After you complete a puzzle, you can check your work with the Solutions that begin on page 53. And remember: all the pictures in this book are fun to color!

Count *all* the dreidels and *all* the Stars of David, wherever they are in the picture.

Help Matthew find his way to the temple.

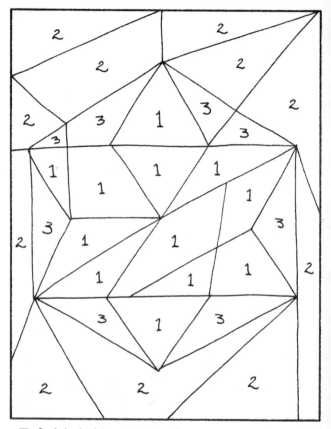

To find the hidden picture, color every space with a 1 in it blue, every space with a 2 yellow and every space with a 3 orange.

How many candles are on the menorah? Circle the
correct number.

Connect the dots to finish the picture.

Find all the objects that do not belong on the sukkah.

Circle the two boys who are dressed exactly alike.

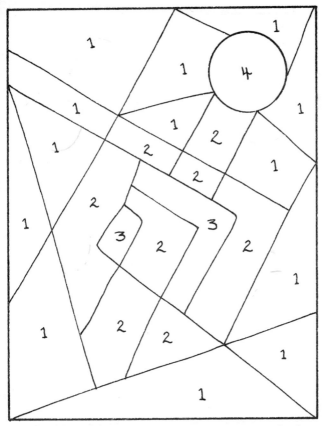

To find the hidden picture, color the 1-spaces pink, the 2-spaces blue, the 3-spaces yellow and the 4-space orange.

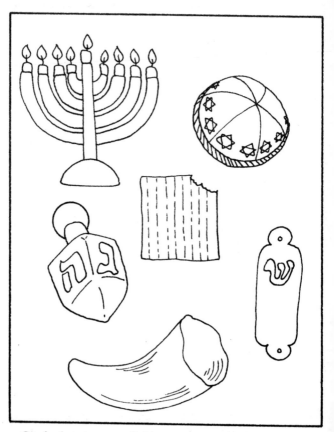

Circle the pictures of objects whose names begin with M.

FINISH

START

Help Noah find the ark.

Find the things in the picture on this page that do not
appear in the picture on the facing page.

Find the five things that do not belong on Noah's ark.

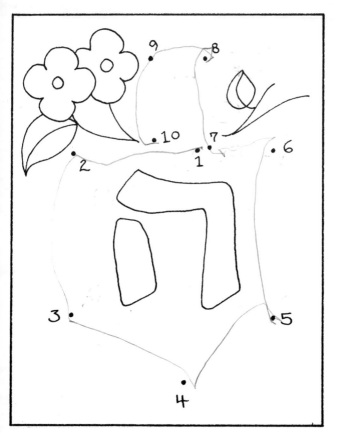

Connect the dots to finish the picture.

Matching up the numbers, fill up the spaces on this page with the names of the four items shown on the facing page. (Words 1 and 4 go down, 2 and 3 go across.)

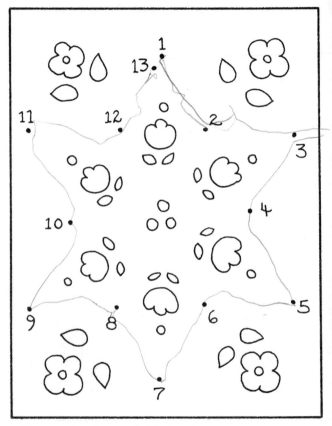

Connect the dots to finish the picture.

Find five things that do not belong on the Tree of Life.

Circle the one crown on this page that exactly matches
Queen Esther's crown on the facing page.

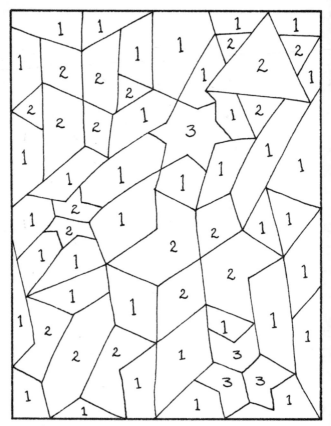

To find the hidden picture, color the 1-spaces blue, the 2-spaces yellow and the 3-spaces orange.

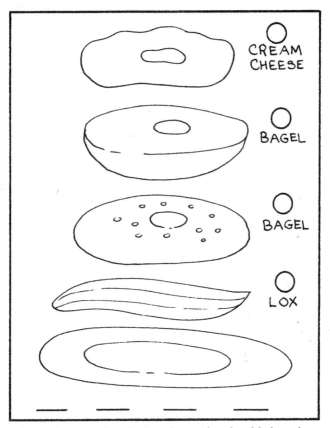

CREAM CHEESE ◯

BAGEL ◯

BAGEL ◯

LOX ◯

To make a sandwich, in what order should these be piled up? Counting the item that should go nearest to the plate as 1, and moving upward from the plate, put the correct numbers in the circles next to the words.

25

FINISH

START

Help Alison get to the menorah so she can light it.

Find the five hidden candles.

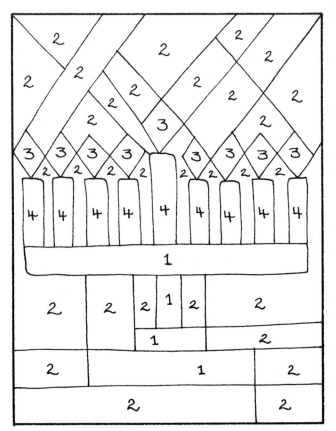

To find the hidden picture, color the 1-spaces yellow, the 2-spaces blue and the 3-spaces orange. Leave the 4-spaces white.

28

Circle the two stars that match exactly.

FINISH

START

Help Daniel find the matzo.

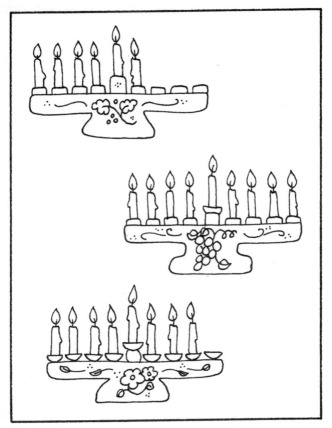

Circle the menorah that has eight candles.

Find the five things on the Tree of Life on this page that are different from the one on the facing page.

Matching up the numbers, fill up the spaces on this page with the names of the four items shown on the facing page. (Words 1 and 2 go down, 3 and 4 go across.)

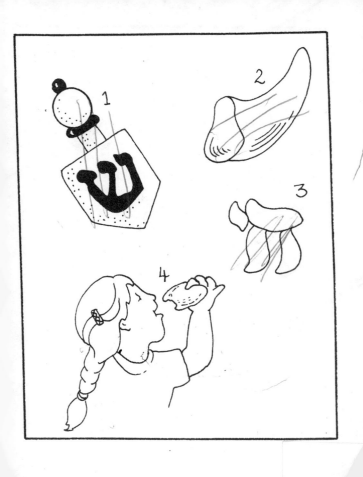

1

2

3

4

Connect the dots to finish the picture.

Find and count the acorns on the sukkah.

Find the things in the picture on this page that do not appear in the picture on the facing page.

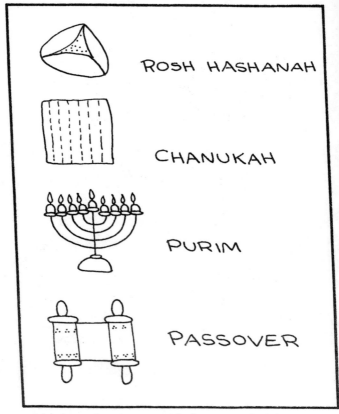

ROSH HASHANAH

CHANUKAH

PURIM

PASSOVER

Match up the pictures with the correct holidays.

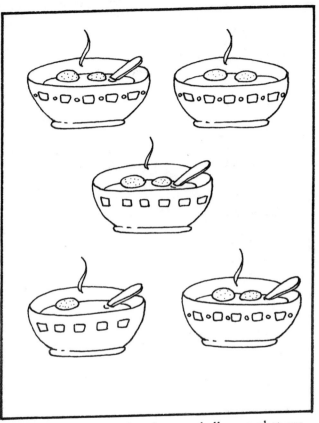

Circle the two bowls of matzo-ball soup that are exactly alike.

Draw a line from each item of food to its place on the Passover plate.

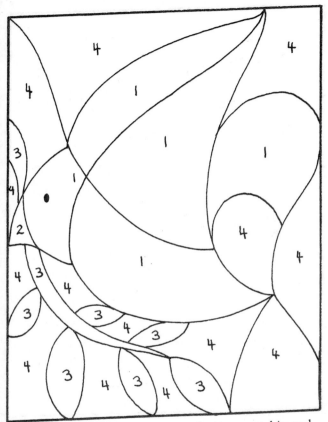

To find the hidden picture, leave the 1-spaces white and color the 2-space yellow, the 3-spaces green and the 4-spaces blue.

RATS

_ _ _ _

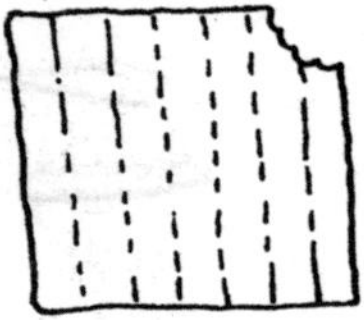

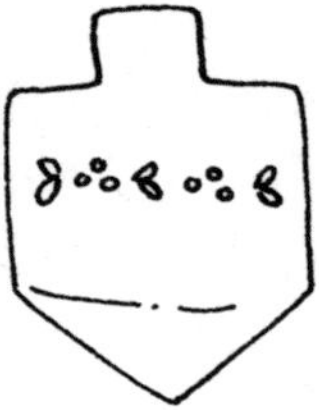

TAZOM

_ _ _ _ _

LIEDDER

_ _ _ _ _ _ _

Unscramble the letters to make words, and match the words with the pictures.

Circle the number of hamantashen that Rayna has baked.

To find the hidden picture, color the spaces with a dot gold and the spaces with an x purple. Leave the spaces with a triangle white.

Aaron is so hungry he's going to eat seven latkes.
Which plate should he pick?

Connect the dots to finish the picture.

Draw a line connecting Ari's dreidel with the one that looks exactly the same.

L	A	M	B	S
I	J	I	E	T
O	C	C	A	H
N	O	E	R	N
S	F	I	S	H

Help Noah find his animals. Look at the names on the facing page and find them hidden in the box above (they can go across or down). When you find them, circle them.

FISH

LIONS

LAMBS

MICE

BEARS

Solutions

page 4 (7 dreidels, 10 stars)

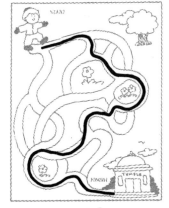

page 5

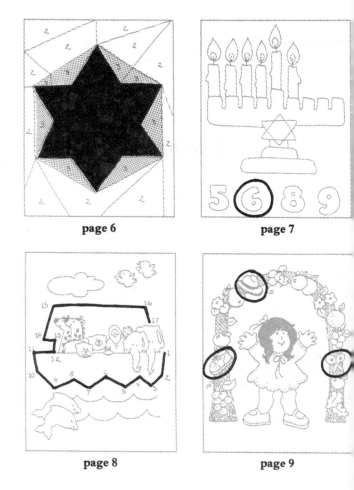

page 6

page 7

page 8

page 9

page 10

page 11

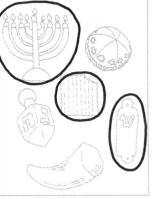

page 12

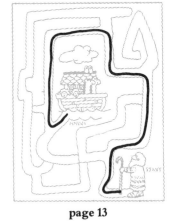

page 13

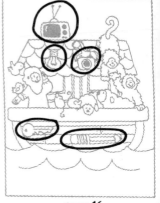

page 14

page 16

page 17

S	T	A	R
	O		
A	R	K	
	A		N
S	H	A	L	O	M
			A
			H

page 18

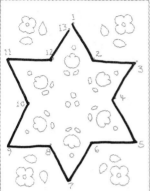

page 20

page 21

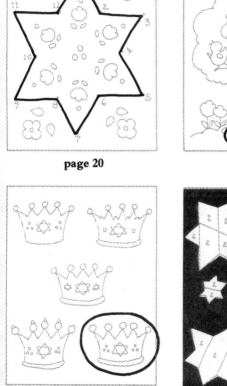

page 23

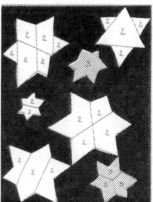

page 24

page 25

page 26

page 27

page 28

page 29

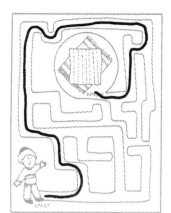

page 30

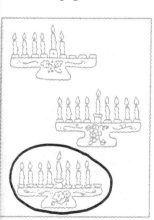

page 31

page 33

page 34

page 36

page 37 (10 acorns)

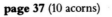

page 38

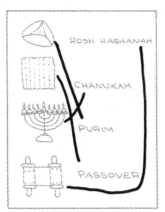

page 40

page 41

page 42

page 43

61

page 44

page 45

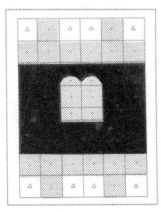

page 46

page 47

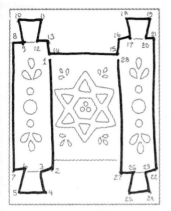

page 48

page 49

page 50